managing
LEADERSHIP

MANAGEMENT SERIES FROM NEW DAWN PRESS

Managing Leadership

Managing People

Managing Sales

Managing Time

Managing Stress

Managing Projects

Managing Text Messaging

managing LEADERSHIP

Y C Halan

NEW DAWN PRESS, INC.
UK • USA • INDIA

NEW DAWN PRESS GROUP

Published by New Dawn Press Group
New Dawn Press, 2 Tintern Close, Slough, Berkshire, SL1-2TB, UK
e-mail: salesuk@newdawnpress.org

New Dawn Press, Inc., 244 South Randall Rd # 90, Elgin, IL 60123
e-mail: sales@newdawnpress.com

New Dawn Press (An Imprint of Sterling Publishers (P) Ltd.)
A-59, Okhla Industrial Area, Phase-II, New Delhi-110020
e-mail: info@sterlingpublishers.com
www.sterlingpublishers.com
www.newdawnpress.org

Managing Leadership
Copyright © 2005 by Sterling Publishers Pvt. Ltd.
ISBN 1 84557 432 X

All rights are reserved. No part of this publication may be reproduced, stored in a retrieval system or transmitted, in any form or by any means, mechanical, photocopying, recording or otherwise, without prior written permission of the publisher.

PRINTED IN INDIA

Contents

Introduction	9
Who the Leader is	14
Leadership Theories	22
Leadership Styles	40
Leadership Skills	44
Qualities in a Leader	71
Some Quotations	95

"A leader is someone who takes the blame for failure but passes the credit to his team," said Dr APJ Abdul Kalam at an informal session with children who had gathered on August 29, 2002 to receive the First Computer Literacy Excellence Award.

Introduction

Why do some companies acquire greatness, and why do not others? The question has become significant as several old business houses are either stagnating or declining. On the other end, many new business houses like Reliance and Infosys are becoming stronger year after year. Though both, the falling and the growing business houses, are functioning in the same corporate and socio-political milieu, why is it that some show a high degree of corporate success and excellence while others prove to be a miserable failure? To find an answer to this problem we talked to several experts and researched in the library. Our conclusion is that the real cause behind success or failure is the leader who is known as the Chief Executive Officer (CEO) of the company.

When we think about the CEO, we are likely to see bold figures and striking deeds. On the international arena, we can locate tall figures like Bill

Gates building a cyber kingdom, Allen Greenspan stewarding a nervous economy, and Jack Walch setting new standards for business performance. Coming to contemporary India two names which fall into this category are: Dhirubhai Ambani, who unfortunately died in 2002, and a living icon, N R Narayana Murty.

Dhirubhai Ambani, who can be called a leader of the twentieth century, proved that Indians could become world class leaders even in a decaying and corrupt system. He grew at a scorching pace to become the head of a company that became the world's largest maker of paraxylene and PET? Not satisfied with that, he set up the world's largest multi-feed refinery. He was not highly educated with high-flying management degrees, but he had a great vision, and understood the minds of men. He could foresee the future needs of the country and the people and followed an audacious but classic business strategy. He believed in three things: making rational decisions, depending on the small investor, and depending on a trusted team of managers.

The greatest success of a leader depends on whether or not he/she is able to professionalise the management and generate the second line of leadership. Most of the Indian CEOs fail in achieving both. They neither professionalise their businesses nor train their successors. Dhirubhai, right from the beginning, picked up the best talent from the market, gave them maximum freedom to operate, and heavily depended on their expertise. Though uneducated in management skills, he sent both his sons to good management schools, and gave them full training in running the business. In fact, all business strategies and tactics were discussed every day at the breakfast table, and the two sons fully absorbed the business acumen of the father. No doubt, the death of the leader did not affect the Reliance business, as it had done in most of the other business houses.

Nagavara Ramarao Narayana Murty is another business leader to prove that it is the institution of CEO, that makes the company a success. As Chairman and Chief Mentor of Infosys Technologies Limited, Murty was wholly responsible for giving the Indian software industry global success. Founded by him along with six others with just Rs 10,000 in 1981, the company was in the limelight within a few years as it was providing high quality software services at low costs. The success strategy of Narayana Murty was threefold. First, he developed healthy relations with the employees, as they were the only ones who were the bridge between the clients and the company. To create a lasting interest in the company he shared the created wealth with his employees. Even his chauffeur is said to have become a millionaire. Second, he generated a true trust in the products and services produced and provided by the company. Finally, he provided the best to the customers so that they never thought of shifting to other organisations. This corporate philosophy resulted in a strong client base that gave high net worth to Infosys.

Good leaders are made, not born. The late Mohan Singh Oberoi is an example of what a CEO can make a corporate entity out of nothing. Oberoi Hotels were nowhere on the scene at the time of independence. Today, his hotel chain is world class and stands amongst the best in the world. He was able to do it because he took care to offer hospitality amidst elegant surroundings to his customers and never compromised as far as quality was concerned. No wonder, Oberoi hotels have built up a regular clientele. When in the post-Asiad period, many of the hotels were facing low occupancy, Oberoi's occupancy rate was pretty high.

P L Tandon is another example to prove that a CEO makes or unmakes a company. Tandon was the CEO of Hindustan Lever Limited (HLL), State Trading Corporation (STC), and Punjab National Bank (PNB). Driven by the growth of the organisation, Tandon developed strong distribution and research systems. With this he was able to transform the three companies and lead them to a new direction. Everyone, at that time, believed that the public sector undertakings were beyond reform and it was not possible to get work done from the highly unionised labour. But Tandon was able to drive everyone, from top to bottom, to work for better results. Unfortunately STC could not maintain the direction, and fell back into a bureaucratic rut. HLL and PNB continued in the new moulds and have been on the progressive path.

What differentiates a good leader from a bad one is the theme we want to discuss in this book. Let us go deeper into the question.

Who the Leader is

There was nothing unusual. A group of children were playing. However, there was a difference. One child was playing the role of a king while others were obeying his orders. The boy was acting like a real king and showing all the qualities of a strong leader. Someone was observing the game being played by the group. He was searching for a leader who could change the shape of the country. The boy was picked up by him and trained for eight years to become an ideal king, popularly known as Chandragupta Maurya.

The person who trained him was Vishnugupta, also known as Chanakya or Kautilya. Chanakya not only trained Chandragupta to overthrow the oppressive and tyrannical rule of the Nandas but also pushed the Greeks out of the Punjab and Sindh. He became a great ruler, one of the most successful kings known in the history, providing the much needed political unity and an efficient administrative system.

Chanakya, solely responsible for the greatness of Chandragupta, can be called one of the greatest leaders in the entire history of mankind. None of the great leaders like Winston Churchill, John F Kennedy, Adolf Hitler, Mahatma Gandhi, Jawaharlal Nehru, Indira Gandhi, Charles de Gaulle, Abraham Lincoln, could attain such feats of leadership as he did.

Chanakya was successful though he had no resources. He rose from ashes and mobilised his own resources to achieve his goal. He came from oblivion with no one backing him. He was born neither with a silver spoon in his mouth nor in a royal family. He converted defeat into victory. He had neither manpower nor money. He motivated and mobilised people to develop a formidable army to defeat the Nandas and the Greeks. He united the country and the society, both of them being highly fragmented. He also developed a political system so good that the empire survived for a long time even after he died. He was not an aggressor, like Hitler or Napoleon. In fact, he fought aggression, exploitation and corrupted power successfully. It can be said that he was such a powerful personality and a catalyst that he changed a weak society into a strong force. None of the above mentioned leaders were able to do what Chanakya did.

Leaders emerge in periods of increasing disorder to become catalysts, change agents, to pull the system out of the disorder. Winston Churchill made the Allies win the Second World War; Franklin D Roosevelt brought the United States of America out of the Great Depression, and Mahatma Gandhi pushed the British out of India.

Who is a leader

It is difficult to define a leader, as it is impossible to define fire. In a five-year period of 1994-99 *Time* magazine, brought out 1,184 articles on leadership. A large number of shelves in all libraries are full of autobiographies of leaders and empirical studies on leadership. It is useless entering into a high profile debate on the semantics of leadership. We, therefore, can, in simple words, say that the leader is a person who leads the team to achieve the targeted objectives. It implies four things:

- A team leader, whose role should be to constantly encourage independent thinking among the team members. They should feel free to approach him with problems for solutions.
- A team comprising members with diverse skills and personalities.
- A definite objective. The team and its leader should know what to achieve. They should know where they have to go. It must set goals it wants to achieve. If that is not done the team will be on a wild goose chase.
- A strategic plan indicating how the resources at the disposal of the team will be utilised to achieve the desired goals in minimum time. It would guide the team's decision making. It would be consistent with the values, purpose, and vision of the leader, and would act as a road map of the programme of action to be taken. It would be a firm indication of how the objectives are going to be achieved. A good plan will anticipate roadblocks by figuring out what could possibly

prevent the success of the plan. It would take care of them in advance of the problem.

Needless to say, a successful leader must have complete control of all the members of his team and the situations he has to handle. The team must accept his commands to work under his directions. Only then he can lead the team to success.

Can You be a Leader

Leadership affects all of us. Whether we work in a hospital, government office, or university, we, in one way or another, supervise other people. Whether we are called upon to be involved in leading government or business, guiding young minds, leading a family, standing for what is right, or organising a dinner, a car pool, or a household, everyone has a leadership role to play. We are each thrust into many different leadership roles again and again, throughout our lives. Our behaviour as a leader has a direct impact on staff performance, productivity, satisfaction, and turnover. Not only are we impacted by it, but we also are all called upon to exercise it.

If leadership is so important and we are liable to play the role of a leader at various stages of life— at home, at office, at playground and in the market—then should each one of us not possess the capacity and capability of becoming a leader?

The answer is a definite YES.

Today the feeling that leadership is a God-given gift has become outdated. Researches on leadership roles and styles have proved that there are no born leaders, as leadership does not depend on luck. It can, in fact, be acquired, as it requires certain competencies and skills that can be developed in a person. An American research group, White Stag, a leadership training institution, has found after prolonged researches that leaders commonly share a definite set of skills and competencies like knowledge, understanding, way of thinking, skills and disposition. If one can acquire these skills one can be an effective and successful leader.

Are Leaders Managers

"Is a leader different from a manager?" is a debatable question for which a definite answer is difficult. Broadly speaking, a leader has a much more important role to play in an organisation than a manager does.

A leader has to transform the organisation and maintain its viability through a continuing process of self-renewal. For that he has to lay down a definite goal and design a strategy to achieve it. A manager, on the other hand, has to achieve the goal by following the strategy. Thus the focus of the two is different. A leader is responsible for setting up the system that takes the organisation to the laid-down goal. A manager is responsible for achieving the goal by implementing the programmes designed by the leader. The role of a leader is to inspire, while a manager has to control the action. The leader's perspective is future, the manager's concern is today, at best tomorrow. A leader fosters innovation, while the manager assigns a high priority to stability. The leader achieves the goal through influence, while the manager relies on formal authority.

No doubt, the role and focus of a leader and a manager are different. But an organisation would gain substantially and enormously if the leader also manages effectively by developing an integrated, systematic and creative approach. The balance between leading and managing can be achieved by 'doing the right things' and 'doing things right'; and having a clear purpose and well-defined processes. Purpose without process causes frustration, and efficient processes minus purpose cause distorted growth.

A high performing organisation will require a person at the top who is both a good leader and an efficient manager.

Therefore, successful managers today also try to acquire qualities of an effective leader. They strike a balance between vertical intuition of a leader and the lateral rationality of the managerial mind. Such persons soon move to the fast lane to reach to the CEO level at a very young age.

This is the reason that good business schools teach leadership skills along with managerial skills to their students.

Leadership Theories

Management experts have studied and conducted researches over the past 100 years to find out what makes a good leader. The earlier theories related leadership with a leader's qualities. Later in the 1950s, leadership effectiveness was attributed to the behaviour of the leader. More recently, it is felt that successful leadership depends on how the leader faces challenges. Here we examine a few leadership theories.

Trait Theory

It is one of the earliest theories, and identifies traits that differentiate leaders from non-leaders. Its focus is on 'what' an effective leader is. The theory believes that a leader must possess certain physical, social and personal characteristics. Physical traits include being young to middle-aged, energetic, tall and handsome. Social background traits mean education at elitist schools and being socially prominent or upwardly mobile. Social characteristics require the leader to be charismatic, charming, tactful, popular, cooperative, and diplomatic. Personality traits include being self-confident, adaptable, assertive, and emotionally stable. Task-related characteristics include being driven to excel, accepting responsibility, having initiative, and being result-oriented.

The theory is not much relevant, as it does not indicate 'how' to lead effectively. Also a study of leaders across the world does not prove any significant correlation between a leader's effectiveness and his personal characteristics. Pope John XXIII was short, balding, stout and significantly older when he was elected the Pope at the age of 76. Within five years he was able to bring about dramatic restructuring and renewal of the Catholic Church that had vigorously resisted any modification of dogma or ritual for centuries.

The trait theory has also not been able to identify a set of traits that can differentiate leaders from followers. It identifies key traits for successful leadership (drive, desire to lead, integrity, self-confidence, intelligence, and job-relevant knowledge), but fails to tell whether these traits are inherent to individuals or whether they can be developed through training and education.

No two leaders are alike. Furthermore, no leader possesses all of the traits. Comparing leaders in different situations suggests that the traits of leaders depend on the situation. Thus, the theory has no takers today.

Behavioural Theory

This theory believes that the primary determinant of leadership is how the leader interacts with the followers. Management experts have given a wide range of leadership styles. Some find leadership as being either political or value driven. Others feel that styles like commanding, manipulating, and patronising are less desirable than a leadership style based on values. A different set of writers suggest that every leader has a different approach to leading: focusing on the future; managing persons differently; championing knowledge; continuing to be conservative; always trying new methods and techniques.

The behavioural theorists have identified certain determinants of leadership so that people could be trained to be leaders. They developed training programmes to change the behaviour pattern of the leader, and believed that the best styles of leadership could be learned.

Theory X and Theory Y

Douglas McGregor described Theory X and Theory Y in his book, *The Human Side of Enterprise*. The two theories represent different ways in which leaders view employees. Theory X believes that employees are motivated mainly by money, are lazy, uncooperative, and have poor work habits. Theory Y, on the contrary, feels that subordinates work hard, are cooperative, and have positive attitudes.

Theory X takes the conservative view that the leader must use authority to direct and control. The assumption is that the average person, by nature, does not want to work, and will avoid it if he can. A worker wants to be directed, wishes to avoid responsibility, has relatively little ambition, and wants security above all. Therefore, the leader must control, direct, and threaten with punishment to make workers achieve the organisation's objectives.

The theory might have been correct in the earlier days of the Industrial Revolution. But in contemporary society its assumptions are so unrealistic that it prevents managers from seeing the possibilities inherent in other managerial strategies. In today's world, if the assumptions of Theory X are put into practice, organisations will fail to discover, let alone utilise, the potentialities of the average human being.

Theory Y is an anti-thesis to Theory X. It has faith in the goodness of an average person and therefore is of the view that individual and organisational goals can be integrated. It believes that a normal person wants to work in the best interest of the organisation. He, therefore, learns, under proper conditions, not only to accept but also to seek responsibility. The majority of workers in a company possess the capacity to exercise a relatively high degree of imagination, ingenuity, and creativity in the solution of organisational problems. It is the failure of the leadership if the intellectual potentialities of the average worker are not fully utilised. Therefore, control and punishment threats are not the only way for pushing them towards better efficiency and productivity. In fact, commitment to objectives needs to be initiated through a function of rewards associated with their achievement.

Theory Y aims at encouraging integration and creating a situation in which an employee can achieve his own goals best by directing his efforts toward the objectives of the organisation. It is a deliberate attempt to link improvement in managerial competence with the satisfaction of higher-level ego and self-actualisation needs. Theory Y leads to a preoccupation with the nature of relationships and the creation of an environment that will encourage commitment to organisational objectives. It would also provide opportunities for the maximum exercise of initiative, ingenuity and self-direction in achieving them.

The Managerial Grid
Robert Blake and Jane Mouton developed a managerial grid model with the help of leadership dimensions identified at the University of Michigan.

It has identified five various leadership styles that represent different combinations of concern for people and production. Managers who scored high on both these dimensions simultaneously (labelled team management) performed best.

The five leadership styles of the managerial grid are: impoverished; country club; produce or perish; middle-of-the road; and team.

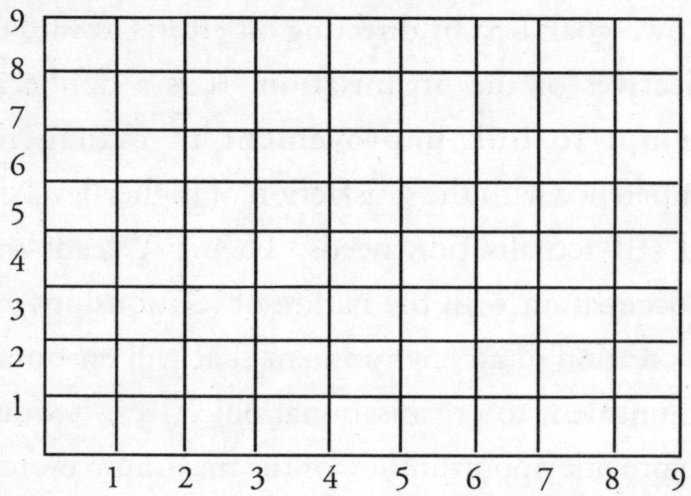

The impoverished style is located at the lower left-hand corner of the grid, point (1, 1). It has low concern for both people and production. The primary objective of this style is for managers to stay out of trouble.

The country club style is located at the upper left-hand corner of the grid, point (1, 9). It shows high concern for people and a low concern for production. The primary objective of the country club style is to create a secure and comfortable atmosphere, and trust that subordinates will respond positively.

The produce or perish style is located at the lower right-hand corner of the grid, point (9,1). A high concern for production and a low concern for people characterise it. The primary objective of this style is to achieve the organisation's goals. To accomplish the organisation's goals, it is not necessary to consider employees' needs as relevant.

The middle-of-the-road style is located at the middle of the grid, point (5, 5). It balances between workers' needs and the organisation's productivity goals. The primary objective of the middle-of-the-road style is to maintain a sufficient level of employees' morale so that the organisation's goals can be achieved.

The team style is located at the upper right-hand of the grid, point (9, 9). It shows a high concern for people and production. This style aims at establishing harmonious relations and fosters a feeling of commitment among workers.

Contingency Model Theory

Fred E Fiedler did pioneering work for 40 years to study leadership and organisational effectiveness. His Contingency Model Theory believes that there could not be the only one best way to lead. Different situations would demand different leadership styles. For example, in a highly routine (mechanistic) environment, where repetitive tasks are the norm (like an automobile factory), a certain leadership style may result in the best performance. The same might not work in a very dynamic environment, like that in an information technology company. Fiedler looked at three situations that could define the condition of a managerial task:

1. *Leader-worker relations*: How well do the manager and the employees get along?
2. *The task structure*: Is the job highly structured, fairly unstructured, or somewhere in-between?
3. *Position power*: How much authority does the manager possess? It measures the amount of power or authority the manager perceives that

the organisation has given him for the purpose of directing, rewarding, and punishing subordinates.

Managers are classified as either relationship-oriented or task-oriented.

Task-oriented managers are more successful in situations that have good leader-member relationships, structured tasks, and power position. The performance would be better when the task is unstructured but the manager holds a powerful position. Also, they do well at the other end of the spectrum when the leader-worker relations were moderate to poor, and the task unstructured.

Relationship-oriented managers do better in all other situations. Thus, a given situation might call for a manager with a different style, or a manager who could take on a different style for a different situation.

These environmental variables are combined in a weighted sum that is termed 'favourable' at one end and 'unfavourable' at the other. Task-oriented style is preferable at the clearly defined extremes of 'favourable' and 'unfavourable' environments, but relationship-orientation excels in the middle ground. Managers could attempt to reshape the environment variables to match their style.

Another aspect of the Contingency Model Theory is that the leader-worker relations, task structure, and the power position dictate a leader's situational control. Leader-member relations are the amount of loyalty, dependability, and support that the leader receives from employees. It is a measure of how the manager perceives them. It also depends on how the group of employees is getting along together. In a favourable relationship the manager has a high task structure, and is able to reward and or punish employees without any problem. In an unfavourable relationship the task is usually unstructured, and the leader possesses limited authority.

The task-motivated style leader takes pride and satisfaction in the accomplishment of the task for the organisation. On the other hand, the relationship-motivated style seeks to build interpersonal relations, and extend extra help for the team development in the organisation. There is no good or bad leadership style. Each person has his or her own preferences for leadership. Task-motivated leaders are at their best when the group performs successfully, such as achieving a new sales record or outperforming the major competitor. Relationship-oriented leaders are at their best when greater customer satisfaction is gained and a positive company image is established.

Hersey-Blanchard Situational Leadership

This theory is based on the amount of direction (task behaviour) and socio-emotional support (relationship behaviour) a leader must provide in a given situation and the 'level of maturity' of the followers. Task behaviour is the extent to which the leader engages in spelling out the duties and responsibilities to an individual or group. This behaviour includes telling people what to do, how to do it, when to do it, where to do it, and who is to do it. In task behaviour the communication is one-way.

Relationship behaviour is the extent to which the leader engages in two-way or multi-way communications. This includes listening, facilitating, and supportive behaviours. The two-way communication can be possible by providing socio-emotional support. Maturity is the willingness and ability of a person to take responsibility for directing his own behaviour. People tend to have varying degrees of maturity, depending on the specific task, function, or objective that a leader is attempting to accomplish through their efforts.

To determine the appropriate leadership style to use in a given situation, the leader must first determine the maturity level of workers in relation to the specific task that he is attempting to accomplish through the effort of workers. As the level of workers' maturity increases, the leader should begin to reduce his task behaviour and increase relationship behaviour until the workers reach a moderate level of maturity. As the workers begin to move into an above-average level of maturity, the leader should decrease not only task behaviour but also relationship behaviour.

Once the maturity level is identified, the appropriate leadership style can be determined. The four leadership styles are telling, selling, participating, and delegating. The telling style is high task/low relationship behaviour (S1). In this style the leader provides clear instructions and specific directions to workers. This style is best matched with a low follower readiness level.

The selling style is high task/high relationship behaviour (S2). The leader encourages two-way communications and helps build confidence and motivation among the employees. However, the leader still has responsibility and controls decision making. The selling style is best matched with a moderate worker readiness level.

The participating style is high relationship/low task behaviour (S3). With this style, the leader and workers share decision making, and no longer need or expect the relationship to be directive. Participatory style is best matched with a moderate worker readiness level.

Low relationship/low task behaviour (S4) is labelled 'delegating'. This style is appropriate for leaders whose workers are ready to accomplish a particular task, and are both competent and motivated to take full responsibility. The delegating style is best matched with a high readiness level among workers.

Path-Goal Model
The Path-Goal Theory developed by Robert House is based on the expectancy theory of motivation.

Taking a lead from the goal-setting theory, it argues that leaders will have to engage in different types of leadership behaviour that would depend on the nature and demands of the particular situation. The job of the leader, according to this theory, is to assist workers in attaining goals. The needed support and direction is to be provided to ensure that their goals are compatible with that of the organisation.

A leader's behaviour is acceptable to workers when viewed as a source of satisfaction and motivation, and the leader facilitates, coaches and rewards effective performance. The Path Goal Theory identifies achievement-oriented, directive, participative and supportive leadership styles. In achievement-oriented leadership, the leader sets challenging goals for workers, expects them to perform at their highest level, and shows confidence in their ability to meet this expectation. This style is appropriate when the worker suffers from a lack of job challenge.

In directive leadership, the leader lets the workers know what is expected of them, and tells them how to perform their tasks. This style is appropriate when the worker has an ambiguous job.

Participative leadership involves leaders consulting with workers, and asking for their suggestions before making a decision. This style is appropriate when the worker is using improper procedures or is making poor decisions.

In supportive leadership, the leader is friendly and approachable. He shows concern for workers' psychological well-being. This style is appropriate when the workers lack confidence.

The Path-Goal Theory assumes that leaders are flexible and that they can change their style, as situations require.

Transformational Leadership

Transformational leadership blends the Behavioural Theory with a little dab of the Trait Theory. Transactional leaders, such as those identified in contingency theories, guide workers to achieve the laid-down goals by clearly indicating the role and task requirements. However, transformational leaders, who are charismatic and visionary, can inspire workers to transcend their own self-interest in the larger interests of the organisation. Transformational leaders appeal to workers' ideals and moral values. They inspire them to think about problems in new or different ways. Leaders can influence workers through vision, framing, and impression management.

Vision is the ability of the leader to bind people together with an idea. Framing is the process whereby leaders define the purpose of their movement in highly meaningful terms. Impression management is the way the leader controls the impressions that workers form about him by practising behaviours that make him more attractive and appealing to them. Research has proved that transformational, as compared to transactional, leadership is more strongly correlated with lower turnover rates of workers, higher productivity, and higher employee satisfaction.

A transformational leader instils feelings of confidence, admiration and commitment in workers. She is charismatic, creating a special bond with workers, articulating a vision with which they identify and for which they are willing work. Each worker is trained, advised, and delegated some authority. The transformational leader stimulates workers, intellectually arousing them to develop new ways to think about problems. The leader uses contingent rewards to positively reinforce performances that are consistent with the leader's wishes. Management is by exception. The leader interferes only when there are problems. He is not actively involved when things are going well. The transformational leader commits people to action and converts workers into leaders.

Transformational leaders are relevant to today's workplace because they are flexible and innovative. While it is important to have leaders with the appropriate orientation defining tasks and managing interrelationships, it is even more important to have leaders who can bring organisations into futures they have not yet imagined. Transformational leadership is the essence of creating and sustaining competitive advantage.

Leadership Styles

If leadership is taking the team to the desired goal, it requires a symbiotic relationship with the team members. The workers expect a certain directional guidance from the leader. The leader, in turn, expects a result from them. Based on this relationship, the leadership style can be of the following types:

Autocratic style
This is the imperial style of leading the team. It was largely followed by the colonial powers. The leader, following this style, does not involve the team members in the decision-making process or the management of the company. The command is centralised and flows downward from the top. Adolf Hitler in the past and Saddam Hussein in the present are the role models of this leadership style. Certain companies in the past, particularly those in the plantation sector, followed this model. Niccolo

Machiavelli in *The Prince* advocated this model when he considered power as a tool, and deemed cultivation of fear to be more important than love.

The management technique used to be simple. The boss told employees what was to be done, and they complied. No one worried if somebody's feelings down the line were hurt. Employees who failed to obey the command were either forced into shape or fired. These authoritarian managers believed that authority should (in a moral sense) be obeyed. Therefore, they expected unquestioning obedience from their subordinates, and they, in turn, submissively obeyed their own superiors.

What could be simpler? Fear ran the work setting. The system was efficient.

The model might have worked in the past but is not acceptable in the contemporary society because true leaders, it is believed, must engage the collective aspirations of the followers.

Puppet Style

Antithesis to autocratic style is the puppet style in which the leadership is not proactive but reactive. Such leaders take orders from their workers or employees and do not have a vision or purpose of their own. The command flows upwards from the worker level. Such leaders are often thrust into their position by accident or because the top leader wants his own henchmen at various positions. Adolf Hitler was, to a large extent, an autocratic leader, and appointed puppet leaders at various positions.

Catalyst Style
In the catalytic style of leadership, the leader is neither a tyrant nor a marionette. In this system the leader and workers form a coherent team and develop an interdependent system. Power is not centralised but is distributed all over the team. Command is given after a careful discussion with certain team players. Followers are empowered to take decisions and work in ways that are not in conflict with the goal and the value system of the organisation. Power flows, like fluid, up and down the organisation, and is amplified by positive feedback. Also known as the Taoist model, it was propounded by the famous Chinese philosopher, Lao Tzu, who in his book, *Tao Te Ching*, describes it as: "When the Master governs, the people are hardly aware that he exists."

The catalyst style is the most popular and successful leadership style for the present-day corporate system. The leader and the employees work in unison to advance the higher needs of the company, while simultaneously retaining their individuality. The team is like an orchestra and the leader like the conductor. A successful chief executive officer will involve those working with him in discussions to inspire them, and bringing out the best from them. He is more of a coach, a mentor or a teacher, and not a slave driver. Such a leader will develop an organisation where every member senses his role, and responds intuitively to the needs of the organisation. Each works with high autonomy while respecting the needs of the overall system.

Leadership Skills

The job of the leader is not just to keep the organisation going. His primary job is to bring dynamism, keeping in view the internal and external changes. The former may be due to the changing aspirations of the workforce caused by the changing business environment. Changing market requirements, new competitive forces and shifting economic, social and technological trends may cause the latter. It is not a simple job that anyone can perform. A set of skills are required that must complement the qualities that a leader possesses. We should know what these skills are before finding out what makes a leader efficient.

Researchers have burnt the midnight oil to find out essential leadership qualities that can apply universally. Though it may be possible to generalise the qualities, cultural differences in various societies must be kept in mind. In fact, cultural influences determine the perceptions and behaviours of the people who accept leaders. As an example, modesty is a virtue in the Netherlands where assertiveness is not an acceptable trait in the leader. On the contrary, assertiveness is a virtue in the United States where modesty will not make a person a great leader. It can be said with confidence that a highly successful leader like Charles de Gaulle of France might not have been acceptable in India, as Mahatma Gandhi would not have become a mass leader in Russia.

Having said that, let us see who are the role models of leadership across the globe.

Who is the role model today? A few names have universal acceptability. Bill Gates is accepted as the undisputed international cyber king, and Alan Greenspan is a known leader in economic management. Mother Teresa was the world leader in mitigating the pain of the poor. Jack Welch has established new standards for business performance. Steven Spielberg is changing the movie-making styles, and Phil Jackson has set new standards for coaching basketball teams in Chicago and Los Angeles. In India, we can identify the late Dhirubhai Ambani, Lal Bahadur Shastri, N R Narayana Murty,

A P J Abdul Kalam, Jawaharlal Nehru and Mahatma Gandhi as universally acceptable leaders. Whenever anyone talks of leadership, images of these leaders come readily to mind, and rightly so.

Focus on the Goal

The primary responsibility of a leader is to set the goal that should be clear and inspiring. Each and every member of the team should accept that and make collective effort to achieve it. The leader should keep the team focused on it. It should, in a way, become the mission for the team.

Goal setting should be the beginning of his responsibility. The leader has to define the goal clearly. The goal gives direction to the team, and creates a trust in the leader that he will be able to lead them to success. It is, however, simple to suggest but difficult to put into practice. More often than not, the leader is not able to put across the goal clearly to every member of the team.

An undefined or confused goal will lack coherent direction. The team will drift aimlessly, and different members of the team will work at cross-purposes. No one will be clear about his role in the whole game, and they would bump into each other, disturbing the whole workplace.

The goal, besides being well-defined and clear, should inspire passion and commitment in each member of the team. Business schools give the example of Phil Jackson who was the coach of the six-time world champion Chicago Bulls. Phil's success was that he kept his team centred on a single, clear, inspiring goal, despite members of the team demonstrating wide range of behaviours. Phil writes about goal setting in his book, *Sacred Hoops*:

"My first act after being named head coach of the Bulls was to formulate a vision for the team ... I started by creating a vivid picture in my mind of what the team could become... I had to take into account not only *what* I wanted to achieve, but *how* I was going to get there.

"My goal was to give everyone on the team a vital role—even though I knew I couldn't give every man equal playing time, nor could I change the NBA's disproportionate system of financial rewards. But I could get the bench players to be more actively involved."

Once the goal is defined and articulated to the team, the team leader has to ensure that the team reaches its goal. It is possible if the objective is not compromised with the vested interests in or outside the organisation. Also the leader has to ensure cordial relationships with the leaders of the other departments in the organisation. Looking for self-gain by the leader causes frustration in the team and the members become demoralised. It causes deviation from the goal, and the whole mission fails. It very often happens in many governmental and political organisations.

Important to achieving the goal is to keep on reinforcing and renewing the goal. If regular communication is not maintained to discuss the goal as the work progresses and modify it in the changing situations then the goal becomes distant. A goal cannot be a rigid and single-minded phenomenon. Markets are ever-changing situations and, therefore, the goal set by the leader in the beginning needs readjustment from time to time.

Modification in goals may be necessary because of either external or internal causes. Several factors may cause changes in the external situations necessitating recasting of the goal. In the early 1970s, the new technology in small calculators reduced the price to one-tenth of the existing price. Today, the technological changes are so fast that no team leader can work on a fixed goal.

Change may also be necessary because of drastic changes in the government policy. The early 1990s witnessed almost daily shifts in the government policy, bringing in more competition and new products. Sometimes, the emergence of a new product shakes the organisation and it has to think anew on its goals. An example is a war between Nirma and Surf or Thumbs Up and Pepsi. The advent of Chinese goods is making the team leaders of most of the Indian companies revise their goals.

Sometimes, the team becomes dissatisfied with its own progress. It happens many a time that the marketing cell created to expand the market share is unable to move forward and achieve the targets. The leader will be under pressure to modify the goal and develop a constructive strategy to regenerate enthusiasm in the team.

Though changing the goal and the direction may be necessary, more important than that is how to

Four factors are essential to cultivate collaborative function in the team. These are openness, supportiveness, action-oriented attitude and positive personality.

Openness means ideas should be exchanged without any fear of antagonising the leader. An effective leader will create a climate where people are free to say what is on their minds. The effective communication and open expression of different points of view will generate an atmosphere in which the problems faced by the team are effectively resolved.

Openness brings about easy communication that is essential for lasting relationships, an important character of a high-quality team. Unfortunately, most of the teams are not able to talk things over. The reason is that team members do not trust each other to disclose the information they have and is needed to solve the problem the team is confronted with. Most of the team members pursue their own agenda, and do not care for the team's goal.

Many a time the behaviour of the leader or important members of the team becomes so degrading and alienating that the team becomes incapable of action.

It is significant to have a successful team with an open communication climate and which, therefore, is capable of dealing with any problem assigned to handle. In a dysfunctional team, members will not be talking to each other easily and openly, rendering the team incapable of dealing productively with any of the problems.

Supportiveness is a desire and willingness to help other members of the team to succeed so that the team's goals are achieved. It means putting the team's goal above any individual agenda, and requires that team members should have a positive attitude. Members work with a team spirit and demonstrate a willingness to help others so that the weaker members are not left in the lurch. At the Indian Military Academy, Dehra Dun, all the cadets have to participate in a crosscountry race before the final term. The winner is not an individual. It is that team whose members reach the winning-post first. The objective is to inculcate a tendency to help the weaker members of the group and to take advantage of one's

action to the leader, experiment with different ideas and do something different. A team lacking action-orientation will consist of members who have passive approach, who wait and hope that others will do something to handle the problem. Such people are not achievement-oriented, and do not rise to the occasion to accept the challenge.

Action-orientation implies job description for each member of the team. As soon as a task is entrusted to the team, the leader assigns specific roles to the different members of the group. In a tradition-driven team persons will be whiling away time and waiting for the orders which they would defy. Each one will work to rule, do the job for which he was employed, and refuse any other work.

Gurucharan Das, in *India Unbound,* gives the example of an action-oriented member of the team, Kamble, who was recruited as the temporary guard at Richardson Hindustan. Within four years he quietly became indispensable for the company.

"First he learnt to operate the telephone switchboard on his own initiative. Next he learnt to use the complicated photocopying machine. Then he began to send faxes. Finally, he became expert in fixing any number of things. He knew who was staying late, who was travelling, how to reach anyone's home. It had got so that if anything was needed after hours, our reaction was, 'Where is Kamble?'

"When our telephone operator went on maternity leave, Kamble offered to take her place for six weeks. We soon discovered that our telephone service had improved dramatically. ...Kamble was too perceptive not to know that our business did not generally come over the telephone, but it was his attitude that mattered."

An action-oriented team would have members like Kamble who believed that action was more likely to succeed than inaction. That is the reason he became so critical to the functioning of the company where he worked. Such persons change the odds in favour of success significantly and dramatically.

Positive personality makes a fundamental difference among people in terms of whether they convey a positive or negative attitude. Positive personality persons get along well with others, and have an infectious enthusiasm about the work. They

The collaborative climate should be utilised effectively in solving problems to achieve goals of the team. Two things are essential for this: the team as a whole, and not only a few members, should participate in reaching the final decision; and, wider discussions should be held before making major decisions. The team must know that good quality results require meaningful problem-solving efforts and arriving at good decisions. The leader should not leave it to chance but guide the team to reach quality decisions. He should create a work environment that promotes productive problem solving. A few things are necessary for this.

First, every member of the team must understand the problem in its true perspective. It is advisable to write down the problems on the board so that everyone focuses on it. Second, all issues related with the problem should be analysed. Third, full information should be made available to the team. The entire discussion should be based on it. Fourth, the judgement should be collective. The leader should discuss important issues with all the members. Consulting only a selected few and communicating the decision to the team will only create a limited trust. However, it does not mean that all the information is to be shared with everyone. The only care to be taken is that members should not feel left out. Lastly, the discussion should be fair and fearless and one should not be intimidated later for opposing the final decision.

Confidence Building

The leader should create a sense of confidence that success would be achieved. "Giving people self-confidence is by far the most important thing I can do. Because then they will act," says Jack Watch, the former CEO of General Electric.

"A leader is someone who takes the blame for failure but passes the credit to his team," said Dr APJ Abdul Kalam at an informal session with children who had gathered to receive the First Computer Literacy Excellence Award on August 29, 2002. Confidence building is intimately associated with achieving results. A passion for winning inspires confidence even among the weakest persons of the team. In fact, once a task has been assigned to a team, there are only two possibilities: the goal may be achieved or it may not be. If team experiences a well-

RS 192,52

belief is not to thank those working under the officer or manager. That was the colonial and imperialistic attitude. The democratic practice is to acknowledge and appreciate team members for their accomplishments. "Good management is nothing more than good manners and common sense. In its simplest form, it's the ability to say thank you," once remarked Karl Bays, the highly successful CEO of American Hospital Supply Corporation.

Knowing the Job
The leader, for effective leadership, must fully understand the technical aspects of the job. Even intelligent, result-oriented and interpersonal skills would not help if the leader lacks sufficient technical know-how. Such a leader may generate frustration in the team, causing falling performance levels and decline in the credibility of the team in the organisation.

Knowing the job implies understanding the content, or body of knowledge, directly related to the achievement of the goal. For example, if the task is to construct a flyover, the leader must understand the basics of civil engineering as applied to a bridge, more specifically a flyover construction. Besides that, the leader should also be conversant with the local conditions, sociology of the population living in the vicinity of the flyover, and the pattern and volume of traffic that would pass over it. In fact, technical know-how is a framework of understanding through which he can identify and analyse key issues related to the team's objective. It is acquired by studying the subject and gaining experience on work. Though the leader need not be an expert in that field, he should be conversant with the key technical issues.

It is impossible for the leader to know all the technical aspects of the work. In today's world, where most of the projects are complex and require interdisciplinary knowledge, it is impossible to find a know-all leader.

Therefore, he has to keep the windows of the mind open, and should freely utilise the knowledge other members of the team possess. Asking intelligent questions, seeking inputs, and willingness to listen and learn can do this. Also he can meet experts and discuss with them significant issues. Such discussions provide invaluable expertise, and he will be able to discuss key topics intelligently. The trust generated among team members would be enormous.

The flow of knowledge, particularly in the information technology sector, in the twenty-first century has been fast. The leader has to constantly update his knowledge and information. If he were out of touch of what is happening in his field of knowledge, he would end up with poor results. Such a leader will be substituted with a better one because organisations cannot compromise with good results.

Clear Priorities

A leader must know what is more important and what is less. He should have his priorities clear, more focused and less ambiguous. If that is not so, the day-to-day functioning of the team will be diffused.

How should priorities be laid down? There cannot be set rules. The guiding principle should be that there should be systematic progress towards the goal.

The need for laying down priorities arises because of finite resources—time, money and energy. Since the resources at the disposal of the team are never adequate, the leader has to decide which of the competing activities is more important. It is not simple, and the final result depends on whether the leader was able to identify the most important activity, and attending it first rather than wasting time and energy on less important ones. A leader who is good in developing an effective priority system is the one who possesses good knowledge of his business, is decisive and confident, and can handle those who do not agree with his decisions.

Once priorities are fixed, it does not mean that these are fixed forever. In fact, in a dynamic society, priorities keep on changing as the work progresses, and the realities of the activity bring forward dichotomy in priorities. However, it should not mean increasing the number of priorities because it may adversely affect the results and the timeframe. Priorities should be changed only when the plan is not working to help in achieving results. And when the change is to be implemented the whole team should be taken into confidence. Reasons for the change should be explained to the team members. It should be ensured that each one understands what the change means. The best way to do it is to ask each team member to address the team to explain the new priorities, and how the changed one would bring better functioning and results. Any change without the approval of the team will cause disruption of the work and discouragement among members.

Performance Management

The final responsibility of the leader is to manage the performance of the team members on a continuing basis. Those who are better performers should be separated from those who are non-performers. Performers should not be treated like passengers. The former should be given responsible and important tasks. The latter ones should be handled carefully. Fair chance and necessary help should be given to improve their performance. If they are not able to do so, they should be shifted or removed.

Managing performance means evaluating the quality and quantity of work done by a person. It implies three things: result-expectation, reviewing results, and rewarding better results.

Result-expectation means that every team member must know what is expected from him. The leader should ensure that each one is clear about the goals and his role in achieving it. The leader should observe the way the member allocates the time and resources while working.

Reviewing results comes next after stated expectations on results. It should be a continuing exercise and not an annual event. The review should be well rounded and shared with the members, and constructive feedback provided to the person concerned. Normally, the feedback is uncomfortable to the person, more so when it is brusque or too critical. One way to diffuse discomfort is to make the feedback unambiguous and as helpful as possible. The leader should be wise enough to know when to be soothing without compromising the message.

The performance problem should not be ignored, and should be handled early enough in a constructive way. The best way to deal with a non-performing member is to call the person to the room and talk in a cool, confident way. It should be explained to him that the achievement of the target is vital for the reputation of the team. The person is also to be told that the reputation and credibility of the company will be affected if he does not perform. Total support should be assured. However, the person should be told firmly, but politely, that in case his performance does not improve he would be replaced with some other person.

Rewarding result is giving recognition to the individual for better performance. The reward should be for something that others have not been able to do or for those results that were not expected from the person. It should not be given for ordinary achievements. Only the excellence, and nothing less than that, should be rewarded. A reward must be meaningful and should make sense. If it does not—to the recipient as well as to others—the reward would not have any value. The whole idea of public acceptance of good work would be lost.

The reward must be just and fair. It should not develop a feeling that it has been given because of the closeness of the person to the leader. It must always be given to a deserving person, and an explanation provided publicly to justify the award.

A person can be rewarded for good work in several ways. A cash prize or promotion can be given. If that is not possible, the person may be appreciated publicly and endorsement made in his personal file.

Qualities in a Leader

Leaders are not ordinary people; they are exceptional human beings who take organisations to higher and higher levels of performance—performance that might not have been imagined before, let alone achieved. Such persons like George Washington, Winston Churchill, Charles De Gaulle, Mahatma Gandhi, Dhirubhai Ambani, etc., must have possessed certain virtues that made them great. What were those hallmarks of effective leadership? Researches on leadership have shown that hallmarks of effective leadership are as follows.

Credibility

The leader should have a high degree of credibility. He must carry the reputation of doing what he says, and doing the right thing. Only credibility gives power to the leader. It was the greatest asset of Mahatma Gandhi on whose one word, millions of people came out on streets and willingly gave their lives. So were many other leaders like Martin Luther King, Jr, and Nelson Mandela. They all won the hearts of the people, as they truly believed what they said.

The leader can gain credibility only by setting examples. It means first doing what they expect from their followers. When Gandhiji wanted people not to buy foreign goods, he himself started wearing *khadi* (cloth made from home spun yarn). In the wake of acute food shortage, Lal Bahadur Shastri gave a national call to forgo one meal in a week. He himself gave up eating dinner on Mondays. Many people still follow his exhortation and do not eat on Monday evenings. Not only does example-setting dictate the success of a leader, but also it teaches tomorrow's leaders how to lead. So set a good example.

Change

The leader has to facilitate change. Change is always resisted and organisational change has 85 per cent mortality. Yet it is the spice of life and is a must for the rejuvenation of any company.

The societies and economies are ever changing phenomena. Organisations too have to change with them. But most of them do not. This causes abnormal, impaired and incomplete functioning of the company. Known as dysfunction, the skill of the leader lies in uncovering it and changing the functioning of the organisation so that it becomes profitable again. Indeed, it is difficult to locate dysfunction in the workplace. It is like locating termite in the house. "You may suspect they're there because you've seen the signs, but don't know where they are or how to get at them," says Tom E Jones, an expert on change management. The leader should have the skill to locate dysfunction and find ways to stop it. Only a change in human relationships, conflict management and corporate culture can overcome dysfunction at the workplace.

Change is widely resisted by dysfunctional workers who fear that their faults will be exposed. Functional employees see change as an opportunity to learn something new, to pick up additional skills, and to become a better person as a result. The success of the leader lies in converting dysfunctional workers into functional ones.

Three critical questions need to be posed before change is formulated: What needs to be changed?

What is the present state of affairs? How it would look like after the change is implemented? If the leader can prove to his team that the change will not bring any harm to them, on the contrary they would benefit, they will appreciate and accept the new work order.

Generally people react to change in three different ways. The first category is of those who are proactive and assertive. They are innovative and respond positively to negative comments, difficult challenges, collective concerns, and personal criticisms. With progressive approach they view change as a way of making improvements within the organisation. They are the ones who solve problems and make things happen.

The second category consists of reactive and aggressive people who have, negative approach about most things and tend to openly resist change in counter-productive ways. Such people avoid responsibility and even indulge in sabotage in thwarting change.

The third group is of inactive and submissive people who go along with change without enthusiasm. These fence sitters accept change when they see it working.

The challenge of the leader is how to handle the second category of people.

In order to bring about a smooth change, William Bridges, in his book, *Managing Transitions: Making the Most of Change,* suggests the leader to follow the following process:

Identify dysfunctional behaviours and understand the impact they are having on the workplace.

Outline and detail the terms of the transition and the changes that are to be brought about.

Identify those individuals and groups who will be the most severely affected by the changes.

The readiness of each work unit to change should be analysed on the following criteria: How is the change being perceived? How well is the change understood and accepted by the people? What is each work unit's openness to the change? Do the people, by and large, support the change? How much of it is understood and absorbed by the grassroots level worker? Are the current behaviour and attitude of the peer groups consonant with the change being envisioned?

Analyse the political implications of these changes.

Set a timebound schedule for each phase of the change.

Set up a team to monitor the progress of the change plan.

Identify the new skills and knowledge required by these changes, and find or develop training and education programmes for those affected.

Retrain dysfunctional workers to develop a positive attitude towards change.

Guide those work units that are resistive to change.

Review the communication within each work unit, and make adjustments as necessary to keep people informed.

Managing Conflict

Conflict is a normal part of the work process—so much so that most of the leaders typically spend 25 per cent of their time dealing with it. Under emergency situations, it is not uncommon for that figure to rise to as high as 80 per cent. With growing competition in the markets, conflict management is of growing importance. The American Management Association (AMA), in one of its survey, rated conflict management "as a topic of equal or slightly higher importance than planning, communication, motivation, and decision making." It also found that conflict management ability would become increasingly important in years to come. It certainly is going to prove true.

Some leaders have negative perceptions of conflict. They believe it to be destructive and therefore want to avoid it. It results in destroying the creative aspects of blending different perspectives. A well-managed conflict-resolution process, in fact, uncovers buried issues, opens up new ideas, and inspires innovation. Conflict provides a natural source of creativity, problem solving, and team building.

A viable conflict-resolution process has to be developed by the leader. It is important to understand the dynamics involved in organisational conflict. Many of the conflicts start small, but become magnified because of several reasons—personal and institutional. Most of the conflicts arise because of differences between the boss and the subordinate or management and employees. The leader should not try to ignore conflict but manage it.

The conflict-resolution process should follow a four-step strategy.

Step one is to track the conflict as soon as its existence comes to knowledge. Significant signs of an emerging conflict are raised eyebrows, caustic comments, unanswered requests, or over-reactions to minor issues. Efforts should be made to find out the viewpoint of the different groups.

The second step is to identify the key players in the conflict. Discuss the causes of the conflict with them. Provide an opportunity to communicate within the organisation. Encourage antagonists to share the basis for their views. Emphasize the value of give and take in the final resolution in the interest of the organisation.

Step three is bringing the conflicting parties to the discussion table. The rules of the game should be set for deliberations and everyone should agree to follow them. Each one should listen to others and understand their point of view. Voices should not be raised and due respect be given to the aggrieved ones. Encourage those who continued to work successfully during the development of the conflict. Focus on what needs to change rather than on who needs to change. If the conflict is not likely to be resolved, try to get an acceptable arbitrator appointed.

Step four is to search for permanent solution. Hurt feelings should be pacified, and the differing groups should try to understand each other's sensitivities. Many rounds of discussions may be needed before a durable resolution is achieved.

Managing conflict involves selecting an appropriate resolution process, building a strategy that meets the organisational needs, blending individual expectations, setting the stage for negotiations, and searching for permanent solutions. It may not be easy, but there is no escape from it. If the leader would not manage the conflict, conflict will manage him.

Problem Solving

A major part of the leader's work consists of solving problems to advance the team towards its goal. Mostly the leaders follow a set pattern of solving problems. It is this: the leader recognises the problem, investigates the cause and decides on a solution that is handed over to the departmental head to implement. The leader following this process invariably does not arrive at the right solution because it is impossible to know the necessary background information.

Rapid, relentless advances in technology and vast amounts of new information pounding at us every day make it impossible for a single leader to know more than the sum of his workers. Each team member's knowledge and his perspectives are essential tools for problem solving. Therefore, it is always in the interest of the organisation to involve the whole team in problem solving. Decisions that incorporate the ideas of a group of people are vastly superior to the single viewpoint of one person imposed on the rest of the group.

A successful leader will create an atmosphere of understanding and awareness by getting the whole team focused on the solution to the problem. First he would understand the nature of the problem and the urgency of resolving it. Then he would assess the availability of information. Finally, he would set a task force of two to four persons to go deeper into the problem and how best to tackle it.

The task force may be asked to work on a four-step strategy.

The first step is to define precisely what went wrong to create the problem. The task force should collect information of what, where, and how it happened, and should identify the most likely cause that created the problem.

The second step is to select the solution. Efforts should be made to decide the action that should be taken. Alternate workable solutions should be finalised and given priorities. Those who would be affected by the alternatives should be asked to provide inputs on various implications of each alternative. After the exercise is intensively done, the solution that is most likely to work should be selected.

The third step is the implementation of the solution. Discussions have to be conducted on what might go wrong. There would be opposition to the action plan, and threats would come from various vested interests. Estimate the probabilities of negative outcomes and how that should be handled. Decide on the authority responsible for the implementation and the reporting of relationships.

The fourth step is the evaluation of the result. At the end of the whole exercise an evaluation should be done. The question to be asked is: "Did the solution work?" and "If it didn't, what went wrong?" The whole experience should be recorded.

The last step is the most important part of the problem-solving process. Normally, when the problem is successfully solved, no one looks back and records the experience. The result is that whenever there is a similar problem there is no benchmark or experience to fall back upon. And if it fails, no one says anything.

Leader as Role Model

The leader is the role model for his team members. They all see in him an ideal person who is to be imitated and followed. He is a sort of a support system as they look towards him in moments of crisis as the solver of all their problems. Therefore, he has to play different roles for his team members. The six roles presented here are the most common expectations from a leader.

Confidence Builder

The leader has to provide encouragement when the team members need a lift. The leader, who is respected by his people, should sense when the spirits of members are low and they need a boost. He should be able to comfort them to get back on track.

Challenger

The team members want someone to question them and suggest a course correction. They need a sturdy sounding board to test their notions, thoughts and ideas. The leader must put demands on their time to listen to him, on their intellect to take him seriously, and on their will power to refute their assumptions.

Motivator

Leaders need to forge and maintain relationships with people to stimulate their thinking and prompt them when they need a reality check. The leader is a starter on an engine—particularly useful when, after a period of idleness, his team needs a quick burst of energy to get moving again. People should be inspired to build up and be progressive. Leaders should provide a positive influence as a motivator.

Perhaps, the single most important technique for motivating the people is to treat them the same way as the leader wants himself to be treated: as a responsible professional. It sounds simple; just strike the right balance of respect, dignity, fairness, incentive, and guidance, and a motivated, productive, satisfying, and secure work environment would be created.

Sustainer
The leader should be concerned for the welfare and well-being of his people. Just like the body, the mind needs nourishment if it is to grow and develop. When the mental health of members sag, they need the leader's help, not just a prop up, but a lift up. The leader should be a person who should be known as one who cares for what happens to his team members.

Friend
The leader should be a friend who cares for his members. All members should be special persons for him. He should respect their point of view, even if they disagree with him. They should feel free to discuss their personal problems and concerns, and easily express their frank opinions. Spending time

with him should provide a type of stimulation that is rarely found in someone else.

Reflector
Team members should aspire to be like their leader in many ways. They value many of the things their leader does. The leader should serve as a "mirror" reflecting the thoughts and feelings of his team members. They should feel comfortable bouncing ideas around in his presence, without fear of judgement or criticism.

Strategist
The art of planning is essential for effective leadership. Good planning involves a sense of strategic direction. What does the team need to do, in a global sense, to get to an established goal? What constraints can be identified, and what can each member of the team contribute?

It must be noted that solid strategies are necessary, but not sufficient in and of themselves, for good planning. Detailed action plans based on those strategies are critically important. The key to effective leadership is how the team members are involved in the development of these action plans. Input should be accepted from all. Everyone should be listened to with an open mind. Those who actually work at the grassroots level can provide invaluable insight into how to get the job done. A consensus should be negotiated, and an action plan finalised on which everyone agrees on who will do what, and by when. Once an action plan is adopted, the leader should ensure that the team has the resources (e.g., funds, equipment, and human power) to execute those plans.

Keen Listener

The image of a leader is that of a talker, giving speeches and not listening to others. Truly speaking, a leader should listen more and talk less. The benefits of good listening are numerous. Relationships improve, productivity and work performance are enhanced, team spirit is fostered, morale increases, and the team gains a better perspective and understanding of the team's mission. Good listening skills engender trust. And trust is what separates effective participatory leaders from autocratic ones.

If the leader listens effectively, the team members would be talking most of the time, say about 80 per cent of the time. The rest of the time, 20 per cent, would be left for the leader to devote asking short, simple questions that draw the person out. What is more, he should ask questions in a concerned, non-threatening style and tone. Good leaders let their workers vent when necessary and acknowledge their feelings.

It is critical that while listening, one should stay open and non-defensive, conveying genuine concern, no matter what the workers say. The attitude while listening should be that the person talking is a team member and wants to improve things. The leader should learn all that possibly can be learnt from the team member so that he is able to address their concerns effectively. A demonstration of concern in resolving problems to their satisfaction not only strengthens the team, but also provides flexibility for the leader when serious problems arise. Past successes build trust, so team members are much more likely to listen to the leader and be reasonable when a problem exceeds his authority.

Accepting Responsibility

Perhaps the most frightening aspect of leadership is that he becomes responsible for someone else's performance. People do things their own way, and sometimes they make mistakes. While team members are responsible to the leader for their mistakes, he is responsible to the top leader for those mistakes. The blame should not be passed down to the team members. It is the leader's responsibility that the members do not commit any mistake. The buck stops with the leader. The team respects the leader's integrity and trusts him to lead. If the leader owns the mistakes of their team members, he becomes a champion, not an oppressor. Harry S Truman, the first post-war President of the United States, had a plate fixed on his desk. It stated: "Buck Stops Here."

Sharing the Spotlight

The flip side of accepting responsibility for everything that goes wrong is giving workers adequate credit for everything that goes right. The leader should not take credit for a team member's work. This would not endanger his career. In fact, his credibility would skyrocket in the organisation if due credit is given to workers. Becoming a leader is in itself the recognition to one's capabilities. The test of his value as a leader is his ability to create a productive, efficient team. If the team is performing at a high level, there is no need for him to blow his own trumpet. His value will be obvious if the team is a high performer.

"Not failure, but low aim is a crime," James Russell Lowell, Professor of Poetry at Harvard University, said more than a hundred years ago. Dr APJ Abdul Kalam, the President of India, endorsed it in his acceptance speech. This is the abstract of what we have discussed. A leader has to aim big. If he does not do that, he would remain a small-time player. Compare Jawaharlal Nehru and Lal Bahadur Shastri with Charan Singh and Chandra Shekhar as prime ministers of India.

An analysis of successful leaders has three common characteristics: they are highly focused, they possess a high level of energy, and they are obsessed. Totally committed to their ambitions, they work relentlessly for hours. They could be called stubborn, even bull-headed, and once an idea has germinated in their minds, they won't give it up.

All said and done, the leader will not succeed if he tries to be a boss. The following poem says it well.

Boss *versus* Leader

The boss drives group members;
 the leader coaches them.
The boss depends upon authority;
the leader on good will.
The boss inspires fear;
the leader inspires enthusiasm.
The boss says "I";
the leader says "We".
The boss assigns the task,
the leader sets the pace.
The boss says, "Get there on time";
the leader gets there ahead of time.
The boss fixes the blame for the breakdown;
the leader fixes the breakdown.
The boss knows how it is done;
the leader shows how.
The boss makes work a drudgery;
the leader makes it a game.
The boss says, "Go";
the leader says, "Let's go."

Test Your Leadership Quotient

It is difficult to find out your leadership strengths or weakness. However, with the help of pioneering work done by John Gardner in his book *On Leadership*, we give here a table of questions to test your Leadership Quotient. General Douglas MacArthur, a brilliant strategist, a farsighted administrator and a successful leader, used these questions to guide him in his leadership duties. These principles can be applied to any leadership situation.

Here is a set of 20 questions. Take your time to respond with either "No" or "Yes" to these questions. Read each question carefully. It is possible that you may have never found yourself in some of the situations described here. Or you may feel that it is not possible to respond in either "No" or "Yes". Nevertheless, imagine yourself in such a situation and *respond honestly*. Your objective should be to find out your strengths and weaknesses, and not to score high points.

Assess your leadership quotient with the help of the scoring table at the end of the following table.

1) Do I heckle my workers?
2) Do I strengthen and encourage them?
3) Do I use moral courage in getting rid of workers who have proven themselves to be unfit?
4) Have I done all in my power by encouragement, incentive and spur to salvage the weak and erring?
5) Do I know by name and character a maximum number of workers for whom I am responsible?
6) Do I know them intimately?
7) Am I thoroughly familiar with the technique, necessities, objectives and administration of my job?
8) Do I lose my temper at individuals?
9) Do I act in such a way as to make my workers want to follow me?
10) Do I delegate tasks that should be mine?
11) Do I arrogate everything to myself and delegate nothing?
12) Do I develop my workers by placing on each one as much responsibility as he can stand?
13) Am I interested in the personal welfare of every

worker, as if he were a member of my family?
14) Have I the calmness of voice and manner to inspire confidence?
15) Am I inclined to irascibility and excitability?
16) Am I a constant example to my workers in character, dress, deportment and courtesy?
17) Am I inclined to be nice to my superiors?
18) Am I mean to my workers?
19) Is my door open to my workers?
20) Do I correct a worker in front of others?

1) No-1; Yes-0.
2) No-0; Yes-1.
3) No-0; Yes-1.
4) No-0; Yes-1.
5) No-0; Yes-1.
6) No-0; Yes-1.
7) No-0; Yes-1.
8) No-1; Yes-0.
9) No-0; Yes-1.
10) No-0; Yes-1.

11) No-1; Yes-0.
12) No-0; Yes-1.
13) No-0; Yes-1.
14) No-0; Yes-1.
15) No-1; Yes-0.
16) No-0; Yes-1.
17) No-0; Yes-1.
18) No-1; Yes-0.
19) No-0; Yes-1.
20) No-1; Yes-0.

Scoring Interpretations

If you have scored between 15 and 20 points, it indicates that you have high leadership qualities. You enjoy successful relationships with your colleagues and superiors. This stems from your ability to trust others, and thus resolve conflicts harmoniously. One of your major strengths is your ability to be aware of emotions both within yourself and others.

If you have scored between 10-14 points, you are an average leader. Most of the time you are able to get along well with your colleagues and superiors, however, at times you may find it difficult.

If you scored between 0 and 9 points, you may be facing problems at work regarding relationships with both colleagues and superiors. You need to cultivate the ability to handle people more carefully. One of the primary factors might be the inability to build trusting relationships, and you must endeavour to be more trusting.

Some Quotations

"Never give an order that can't be obeyed."
General Douglas MacArthur

"Great leaders are almost always great simplifiers, who can cut through argument, debate, and doubt to offer a solution everybody can understand."
General Colin Powell

"Men make history and not the other way around. In periods where there is no leadership, society stands still. Progress occurs when courageous, skillful leaders seize the opportunity to change things for the better."
Harry Truman

"The final test of a leader is that he leaves behind him in other men, the conviction and the will to carry on."
Walter Lippmann

"People ask the difference between a leader and a boss. The leader leads, and the boss drives."

Theodore Roosevelt

"Four rules of leadership in a free legislative body:

"First, no matter how hard-fought the issue, never get personal. Don't say or do anything that may come back to haunt you on another issue, another day...

"Second, do your homework. You can't lead without knowing what you're talking about...

"Third, the American legislative process is one of give and take. Use your power as a leader to persuade, not intimidate...

"Fourth, be considerate of the needs of your colleagues, even if they're at the bottom of the totem pole..."

*George Bush, Former President
of the United States*

"Speak softly and carry a big stick; you will go far."

Theodore Roosevelt